I Fell Out of Bed

Written by Miriam Simon
Illustrated by June Goulding

I fell out of bed
and bumped my head.

I went downstairs
and saw three bears.

4

I put on my mittens
and saw three kittens.

I opened the cupboard
and saw Mother Hubbard.

I looked up the hill
and saw Jack and Jill.

I sat on the swing
and saw a king.

I rubbed my head

and went back to bed.

I fell out of bed
and bumped my head.
I went downstairs
and saw three bears.
I put on my mittens
and saw three kittens.
I opened the cupboard
and saw Mother Hubbard.
I looked up the hill
and saw Jack and Jill.
I sat on the swing
and saw a king.
I rubbed my head
and went back to bed.